A Tribute to
THE YOUNG AT HEART

GWENDOLYN BROOKS

By Jill C. Wheeler

Published by Abdo & Daughters, 4940 Viking Drive, Suite 622, Edina, Minnesota 55435.

Copyright © 1997 by Abdo Consulting Group, Inc., Pentagon Tower, P.O. Box 36036, Minneapolis, Minnesota 55435 USA. International copyrights reserved in all countries. No part of this book may be reproduced in any form without written permission from the publisher.

Printed in the United States.

Cover and Interior Photo credits: Wide World Photos
Bettmann Archives

Edited by Julie Berg

Library of Congress Cataloging-in-Publication Data

Wheeler, Jill, C., 1964—
      Gwendolyn Brooks / Jill C. Wheeler.
            p. cm. -- (A Tribute to the Young at Heart)
      Includes index.
      Summarry: A biography of the African-American poet who won the Pulitzer
Prize in 1950 and whose poems reflect the experiences of African-Americans.
      ISBN 1-56239-786-9
      1. Brooks, Gwendolyn, 1917- --Biography--Juvenile literature. 2. Afro-
American women poets--20th century--biography--juvenile literature. [1.
Brooks, Gwendolyn, 1917- 2. Poets, American. 3. Afro-Americans--Biography.
4. Women--Biography.] I. Title. II. Series.
PS3503.R7244Z99   1997
811'.54--dc21   96-29806
[B]   CIP
                                           AC

Table of Contents

I DON'T BELIEVE IT!

Each spring Columbia University presents the Pulitzer awards. These prestigious awards honor people who have excelled in journalism. The awards also recognize people in other types of writing, such as fiction and poetry. Few honors are as important as a Pulitzer Prize.

The Pulitzer committee just had awarded the prizes on May 1, 1950. Poet Gwendolyn Brooks didn't know it. She, her husband, and son were sitting in their apartment on Chicago's famous South Side. All the lights were off because the family could not pay the electric bill. Then the phone rang.

When Gwendolyn picked up the phone, she found herself talking to a reporter with the *Chicago Sun Times*. "Do you know you have won the Pulitzer Prize?" he asked. With that, she realized she had become the first African-American ever to receive that honor.

Opposite page: Poet, Gwendolyn Brooks, at the Library of Congress, 1985.

"I don't believe it!" she shouted. She grabbed her son and they danced around the room. Later they all went to a movie to celebrate.

It was a quiet celebration for such an honor. Yet Gwendolyn Brooks had never been one to make a big deal out of things. "It is wonderful to have awards," she said. "But you don't live for awards. You do your work as best as you can and enjoy it. That's what is most important."

Even though Gwendolyn doesn't seek awards, she has received more than her fair share. In addition to the Pulitzer Prize for poetry, she has received many honors for her poetry, fiction, and nonfiction. She holds 15 honorary doctorates. People at colleges and universities around the nation frequently ask her to lecture on their campuses.

Many people would say Gwendolyn has succeeded as a poet because she was born to be one. She disagrees. "I'd say this to anybody passing in the street. 'You are a poet.'

Everybody is a poet. I mean by that, all of us have deep feelings."

"The only difference is that the others keep walking on down the street," she adds. "Poets bother to put these things down on paper."

Gwendolyn has been putting her poems down on paper since she was seven years old. Since then, she's published more than 15 books of poetry, fiction, and nonfiction. Many magazines also have published her work. She remains one of America's most famous poets. She also credits much of her success to the support of her family over the years.

Gwendolyn Brooks with her book, *A Street in Bronzeville.*

HUMBLE BEGINNINGS

Gwendolyn Brooks was born on June 7, 1917, to David Anderson and Keziah Wims Brooks. David was the first in his family to finish high school. His father had been a slave. David studied a year at Fisk University to be a doctor. Unfortunately, he could not afford school and a family.

David became a janitor for a music publisher in Chicago. He earned $25 a week. Then the Depression took hold. The Depression was a time when many companies went out of business. Hardly anyone had money. David's salary dropped to just $10 a week during the Depression. He painted stores and apartments at night to earn extra money for his family.

Those days were tough for the Brooks family. The family struggled to find enough money to get by. Yet there were bright spots, too. Once David found an old desk that he gave to his daughter. Young Gwendolyn loved the desk. It had many compartments and long drawers. She could store her books in it.

Gwendolyn loved her many books. So did the rest of her family. They all loved to read and write. Keziah had been a schoolteacher in Topeka, Kansas, before her marriage. Both parents strongly supported education and books.

They also believed literature was important. David often sang around the house and read poetry. Gwendolyn loved to hear him recite the poems of Paul Laurence Dunbar and other classics. Paul Laurence Dunbar was a popular African-American poet of the time. The Brooks family loved his work. Gwendolyn wanted to write poetry that was as beautiful as Dunbar's was.

When Gwendolyn was seven years old, she brought her mother a page of rhymes she had written. "She was immediately impressed," Gwendolyn recalled. "She said I was going to be the lady Paul Laurence Dunbar. That black poet was our household idol, so it meant a lot for her to say that."

Gwendolyn took her mother's words to heart. She wrote almost constantly. Her poems were about her friends, her enemies, and nature. She would rather write than play with friends. Once there was a fire down the block. Gwendolyn's family ran outside to see what was happening. Gwendolyn ignored the fire and continued to write. She believed it was her calling.

"From the very beginning I felt that was my destiny, to be a writer," she said. "I'd often write two, three, five poems in a day. I enjoyed it."

"I remember once I got angry. I was about 13 or 14 and tore up a story I had written. I don't know what I was mad about. But this was about the worse thing that anybody could do, according to my father. 'You tore up the story, Gwendolyn?' he asked in horror. I had that kind of support behind me all the time."

PROMISING YOUNG POET

Gwendolyn surprised many people with her verses. Some of her teachers didn't believe Gwendolyn had written them. They accused her of stealing the poems.

"They felt the little compositions I wrote couldn't be mine," she said. "They were sure I was copying from someone." That made Gwendolyn angry. It made Keziah even angrier. She would race down to the school. She would tell the teacher her daughter had talent. Gwendolyn didn't need to steal anyone else's work, she told them.

Gwendolyn published her first poem when she was just 11. It was in her neighborhood newspaper. When she was 13, she published a poem in a magazine called *American Childhood*. The magazine sent her six copies of the issue as payment for the poem. She also published a neighborhood newspaper and sold it for five cents a copy.

These successes inspired Gwendolyn. She found a book called the *Writer's Market*, which listed all kinds of publications. The book also tells what writings those publications are likely to publish. Gwendolyn would submit her work to different publications. Then she would wait to hear back from them. Sometimes it was good news. Most of the time the publications rejected her work. Yet she didn't stop trying.

At age 16, she sent some of her best poems to African-American writer, James Weldon Johnson. He wrote back and said her poetry was good. However, he said she needed to work on it a little more. He suggested she read poetry other people had written. Gwendolyn followed his suggestion and began reading the works of Ezra Pound, T.S. Elliot, and e.e. cummings.

Gwendolyn also had a chance to meet an African-American poet named Langston Hughes. She had read much of his work. One day at Chicago's Metropolitan Church, she had the chance to show him some of her poems. He said she had a lot of talent and should write more. The two kept in contact from then on. Years later, Hughes would dedicate one of his books of poetry to Gwendolyn.

Meanwhile, Gwendolyn remained dedicated to poetry. She even made a list of New Year's resolutions in 1934. Her top resolution was "Write some poetry every day."

African-American poet, Langston Hughes.

LIFE IN THE MECCA

Gwendolyn graduated from Chicago's Englewood High School in 1934. Then she enrolled at Woodrow Wilson Junior College for two years. She continued to write as she had resolved. She was a regular contributor to the Chicago *Defender*. It was the local African-American newspaper.

After graduation, it was time to find a job. Gwendolyn began taking jobs cleaning and doing other domestic work. It was all that was available. The country was still struggling to get out of the Depression. Yet the domestic jobs were hard and made her feel badly about herself.

Finally, Gwendolyn found a more permanent job. She was one of five typists for a "spiritual advisor" who lived in the Mecca Building. The Mecca was a huge apartment complex in Chicago. Gwendolyn's job was to answer letters people sent to the advisor. People would ask the advisor questions about what to do with their lives. "We were like Ann Landers," Gwendolyn recalls.

Other times, Gwendolyn and the others sent things to people. They filled little boxes with brightly colored powders and filled bottles with liquids. They delivered these potions to residents in the Mecca. The residents believed the potions would help them with their problems.

Gwendolyn didn't like her job. She thought the advisor was dishonest. She believed he was taking advantage of people. Yet she needed the money from her job. She made $8 a week. She gave $2 of her salary to her family each week. Finally Gwendolyn's boss asked her to do some preaching. She refused. He fired her.

Years later, Gwendolyn would write a poem called "In the Mecca." It talked about the lives of the people who lived there.

Gwendolyn Brooks, age 32, after winning the Pulitzer Prize.

FIRST COMES LOVE ...

During her work at the Mecca, Gwendolyn became involved in a special group. It was the NAACP Youth Council. The NAACP is the National Association for the Advancement of Colored People. The Youth Council was a special group for young African-Americans. Many of the members were writers like Gwendolyn.

The group gave Gwendolyn a chance to blossom. She had always been shy and kept to herself. Now she became more outgoing and met more people. One of them was a young man named Henry Blakely. Henry had heard that the Youth Council included a young woman who wrote poetry. Henry also wrote poetry. He wanted to meet the young woman who shared his passion for words.

Opposite page: Charles H. Houston, President of the NAACP at the time Gwendolyn Brooks was involved with the organization.

16

Gwendolyn remembers well the first time he came to the Council. She was sitting in the local YWCA with a friend. She saw a man walk in. Later she said he looked distinguished. Gwendolyn told her friend, "There is the man I'm going to marry." It was Henry Blakely.

That's exactly what she did two years later on September 17, 1939. The newlyweds settled down into a tiny kitchenette apartment. Life in the apartment was cramped and bleak. Yet it was all they could afford. Money was tight. Henry found a job working for an insurance firm. He never knew how much money he would make. He earned his salary when he sold insurance to people. When money was tight, many people dropped their insurance. Henry lost out then, too.

Gwendolyn and Henry's lives changed forever on October 10, 1940. Gwendolyn gave birth to a baby boy. The couple named him Henry Jr. Now there was another mouth to feed. Henry found a different job as a driver/salesman for a soft-drink company. Then he took a job with a defense contractor.

The family moved again. They settled into a tiny kitchenette apartment with mice and a shared bathroom. Gwendolyn took a one-year break from writing after Henry Jr. was born. In 1941, she was ready to dive in again.

A BOOK AT LAST

In 1941 Gwendolyn met a woman who would change her life yet again. Inez Cunningham Stark loved poetry. She was white. She also believed African-Americans needed more opportunities to write poetry. She organized a workshop for African-American poets in a community center on the south side of Chicago. She had 15 students in her class. They included Gwendolyn and Henry.

The students commented on each other's work. Inez critiqued their work as well. Gwendolyn learned many things from Inez's comments. She learned that every word in a poem had to matter. Sometimes the criticisms were harsh. Gwendolyn didn't mind.

"Young people these days say they get discouraged," she said in an interview years later. "That's a foreign language to me. I never was discouraged. And that was because I enjoyed what I was doing. Even if I had known that I was never going to get anywhere, poetry was something I loved doing."

Gwendolyn enrolled in a poetry writing class at Northwestern University soon after the workshop. The class helped her write better poems. One of her poems won the poetry prize at the Midwestern Writer's Conference in 1943. An editor representing a major publishing company was at the conference. She heard about Gwendolyn's prize-winning poem. She asked Gwendolyn if she had enough poems for a book. Gwendolyn sent Knopf 40 of her poems. The editor sent them back.

Gwendolyn took 20 of the 40 and sent them to a different publisher, Harper & Brothers. Harper wrote back asking for more poems so they could publish a book. The news thrilled Gwendolyn. She gave up going to movies and parties so she could write instead. She wrote 12 new poems and sent them to Harper.

Like most of her work, the poems were stories of real people. They talked about what it was like to be African-American in the city. They talked about childhood, marriage, and God. Harper accepted the poems for publishing. Gwendolyn would soon have her book!

"I can really recall that moment, after wanting it for so long," Gwendolyn recalled. "You know, that's all I wanted to do in my life. Publish a book of poems. Just one book is all I wanted."

That book was *A Street in Bronzeville*. It brought national attention to poet Gwendolyn Brooks.

Gwendolyn Brooks while working on her poetry.

PATHWAY TO A PULITZER

Immediately, Gwendolyn set out to write a new book. She wanted this one to be even more beautiful than the first. "I wanted every phrase to be beautiful," she said. "I was very conscious of every word. Every one was worked on and revised, tenderly cared for. More so than anything else I'd written. Some of it just doesn't come off. But it was enjoyable."

Gwendolyn sent Harper her new book of poems and waited. Finally, she heard from them. They had sent the poems to another poet to read. That poet didn't like many of the poems and wanted others changed. Gwendolyn refused to change anything. In 1949, Harper published the book the way Gwendolyn wanted it. She called it *Annie Allen*. It was about African-American life in Chicago.

Annie Allen quickly gained national attention as well. In 1950, Gwendolyn won the Pulitzer Prize for poetry for the book. She was glad she had insisted the poems stay as they were. "I'm afraid I was a little nasty at that point," she said. " 'You see?' I pointed out. 'I was right!' Harper never submitted any of my poems afterward for somebody to read — or if they did, I was never told."

Meanwhile, Gwendolyn had another important project. Her daughter, Nora, was born in 1951. Unlike before, Gwendolyn kept on writing after the baby's arrival. "When Henry was a baby, I wrote when he was asleep. When he was older, I would write when he was in school," Gwendolyn recalled. "When Nora came, she was such a lovely baby. She gave me no trouble whatsoever. She would take her nice little naps. And I would write. We'd go out to the park, sometimes. I at least would be able to make notes, think of phrases that I might be able to use."

Two years after Nora's birth, Gwendolyn published a novel, *Maud Martha*. *Maud Martha* is the story of an African-American girl growing up on Chicago's South

Side. Three years later, Gwendolyn published a children's book of poems. She called it "Bronzeville Boys and Girls."

Gwendolyn also was paying more attention to the world around her. In the 1950s, many people frequently treated African-Americans unfairly. It was harder for African-Americans to find good jobs than it was for white people. It was harder for them to find decent places to live than for white people. All of that was simply because they were African-American.

That had always bothered Gwendolyn. Now she decided she wanted to do more about it.

A NEW VOICE FOR AFRICAN-AMERICANS

Gwendolyn began writing poems about what it was like to be African-American in the United States. The poems spoke of the anger and despair many African-Americans felt. Some of the poems grew out of stories Gwendolyn heard on the news. One was the story of Emmett Till, a 14-year-old African-American boy. He was murdered because he had spoken to a white woman.

That poem and others went into her next book. She called it *The Bean Eaters*. It was published in 1960. At first, few people talked about the book at all. Then they began to complain. They said it talked too much about social problems. The book included one of her most famous poems. It's the sad story of seven young pool players. The title is "we real cool."

Shortly after *The Bean Eaters* came out, Gwendolyn began to teach. She taught creative writing at several colleges and universities in the area. "I tried very hard not to get my students to write like I do," she said. She also advised would-be poets to "tell your reader less. Let him do a little digging."

In spring 1967, Gwendolyn attended a Black Writer's Conference at Fisk University. She met many people who inspired her. She heard them say that African-American poetry is by African-Americans, about African-Americans, to African-Americans. Gwendolyn vowed to write poems that talked about her pride in being black.

Years before, Gwendolyn had started writing a novel. It was about the events she'd experienced while working in the Mecca Building. She reviewed the material, then wrote poems about it. The result was another book called *In the Mecca*.

Once again, people criticized Gwendolyn for *In the Mecca*. They said it was written only for African-

Americans. She defended her work. "I want to speak more and more effectively to black people. All kinds of black people. My address, since 1968, has been to blacks because there is just so much I have to say to them," she said.

"Real poetry comes out of the mouths of the street," she added. "In my poems I want to include music, imagery, picture, philosophy, lyricism, humor. But I want to offer them to people who may not have been able to go to college."

Emmett Till, the 14-year-old youth who was shot and whom Brooks wrote about.

SUPPORTING AFRICAN-AMERICAN POETRY

Even as she wrote about the African-American experience, Gwendolyn had another mission. She wanted to get more African-Americans to write their own poetry. She began by organizing a writer's workshop. She invited members of the Blackstone Rangers, a street gang. She talked to any African-American poet who would listen.

"We would go around to the parks, to the taverns, to Cook County jail even and read our poems," she said. She and her friends chose poetry that spoke to the real lives of their listeners. "You have to speak to them in terms that seem relevant to what they know of life. You have to have a poem that they can take to immediately."

Gwendolyn had another chance to help young African-American poets in 1969. Illinois named her poet laureate for the state. The state gives the honor to just one resident each year. Ever since then, she has been sponsoring an annual poet laureate contest. The contest recognizes outstanding poets in elementary and high school.

Gwendolyn also made a difficult decision. Harper's had been her publisher for many years. Yet she felt it was important to support publishers owned by African-Americans. She decided to switch her work to Broadside Press. She liked the way Broadside published new voices of African-Americans.

Gwendolyn still receives questions and letters from young poets. Many ask her what they should do to become better poets. "Read, read, read," she tells them. "Write, write, write. Live, live, live. Don't be afraid to think for yourself. Be yourself."

WRITINGS

Following is a listing of some of Gwendolyn Brooks' writings. Check them out to get to know one of America's premiere poets.

A Street in Bronzeville, Harper, 1945

Annie Allen, Harper, 1949

Maud Martha, Harper, 1953

Bronzeville Boys and Girls, Harper, 1956

The Bean Eaters, Harper, 1960

Selected Poems, Harper, 1962

In the Mecca, Harper, 1968

Riot, Broadside Press, 1969

Family Pictures, Broadside, Press, 1970

Aloneness (poetry), Broadside Press, 1971

Jump Bad, Broadside Press, 1971 (editor)

A Broadside Treasury, Broadside Press, 1971

Report from Part One: An Autobiography, Broadside Press, 1972

The Tiger Who Wore White Gloves, or What You Are You Are, 1974

Young Poet's Primer (1980)

Very Young Poets (1983)

GLOSSARY OF TERMS

Columbia University — a famous university in New York City.

Depression — the time following the United States' economic crash of 1929. Most people had very little money then.

Honorary doctorate — an honor given by universities to certain successful people.

National Association for the Advancement of Colored People (NAACP) — an organization that seeks to help African-Americans.

Poet laureate — a special honor given to a poet from a particular state or country.

Pulitzer Prize — a special honor given each year to different types of writers.

Index